D1278374

Take Care of Yourself

Keeping Clean

Siân Smith

Chicago, Illinois

www.capstonepub.com

Visit our website to find out more information about Heinemann-Raintree books.

To order:

 Phone 800-747-4992

Visit www.capstonepub.com to browse our catalog and order online.

Edited by Dan Nunn, Rebecca Rissman, and John-Paul Wilkins
Designed by Victoria Allen
Picture research by Tracy Cummins
Production by Alison Parsons
Originated by Capstone Global Library Ltd
Printed and bound in China by Leo Paper Products Ltd

16 15 14 13 12
10 9 8 7 6 5 4 3 2 1

Library of Congress Cataloging-in-Publication Data
Smith, Siân
  Keeping clean / Siân Smith.
    p. cm.—(Take care of yourself!)
  Includes bibliographical references and index.
  ISBN 978-1-4329-6709-3 (hb)—ISBN 978-1-4329-6716-1 (pb)
1. Hygiene—Juvenile literature. I. Title.
RA780.S56 2013
613—dc23
                          2011049838

Acknowledgments
We would like to thank the following for permission to reproduce photographs: Capstone Publishers pp. 8, 21 (Karon Dubke); Corbis pp. 7 (© Image Source), 13 (© Rubberball); Getty Images pp. 10 (Jae Rew), 11 (Nick White), 12 (Fuse), 20 (Kohei Hara); istockphoto pp. 15 (© David Hernandez), 16 (© jianying yin), 17 (© Eric Michaud); Shutterstock pp. 4 (© Gorilla), 5, 9 (© Monkey Business Images), 6 (© 3445128471), 14 (© Catalin Petolea), 18 (© kondrytskyi), 19 (© Boris Sosnovyy), 22a (© Tina Rencelj), 22b (© Niki Crucillo), 22c (© terekhov igor), 22d (© Nitr), 23a (© Loskutnikov), 23b (© Grandpa).

Front cover photograph of a young girl in a bathroom wrapped in towels reproduced with permission of Getty Images (LM Productions). Rear cover photograph of child's hands covered in soap reproduced with permission of Shutterstock (© 3445128471).

Every effort has been made to contact copyright holders of material reproduced in this book. Any omissions will be rectified in subsequent printings if notice is given to the publisher.

We would like to thank Nancy Harris and Dee Reid for their assistance in the preparation of this book.

Contents

Keeping Clean

Everyone needs to keep clean.

Keeping clean helps you to
stay healthy.

Washing Your Hands

Wash your hands with soap and water.

Wash your hands all over.

Wash between your fingers, too.

You need to wash your hands
after you go to the bathroom.

You need to wash your hands
before you eat.

Changing Your Clothes

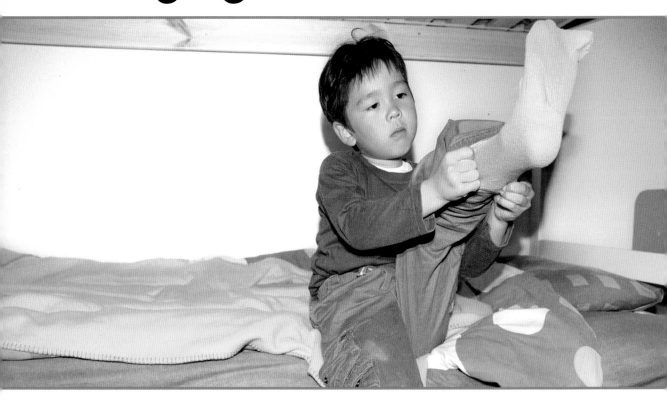

Put on clean underwear and
socks every day.

Change your other clothes often.

Don't wear clothes if you know
they are dirty.

Put them in the laundry
basket instead.

Keeping Your Body Clean

Wipe your nose with a tissue.

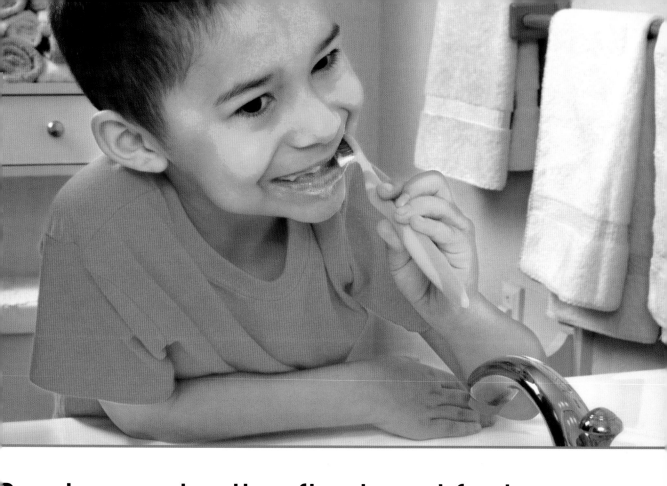

Brush your teeth after breakfast.
Brush your teeth before you sleep.

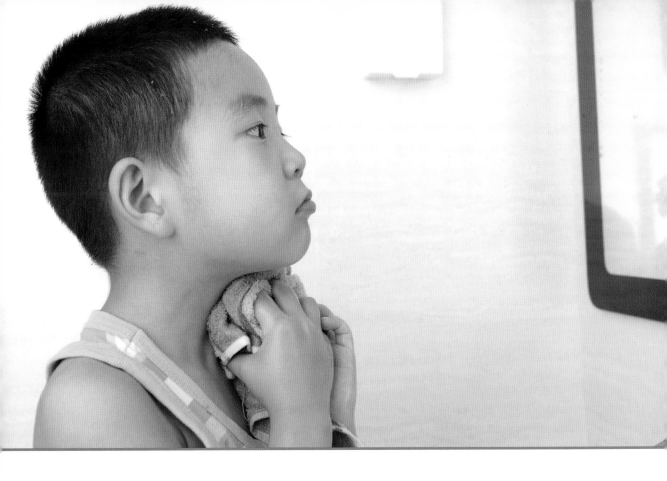

Wash your face when it gets dirty.
Wash your face before you sleep.

Take a bath or a shower every
day if you can.

Clean your body with a washcloth and soap.

Clean your hair with shampoo.
Then wash the shampoo away.

Make sure you clean everywhere.

Dry your body everywhere, too.

Name Game

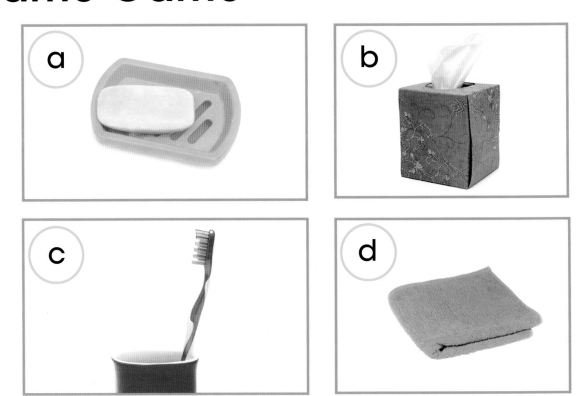

Can you name these things?

They help you to keep clean.

Answers on page 2

Picture Glossary

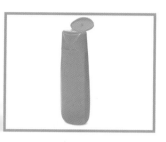

shampoo special soap you use to wash your hair

underwear clothes you wear next to your skin, under your other clothes

Index

Answers to question on page 22
a = soap   b = tissue
c = toothbrush   d = washcloth

Notes for parents and teachers
Before reading
Brainstorm things we do to keep our bodies healthy. Encourage the children to think about the importance of exercise, sleep and rest, eating and drinking well, and keeping our bodies clean and safe.

After reading
- Draw or place a picture of a person on the board and draw lines to their hair, nose, teeth, hands, and feet. Ask the children what we do to keep each of these body parts clean. Record this by writing or drawing a picture to go with each label. What do we do to keep our whole body clean?
- Children can take turns in miming something they do to keep their body clean for the others to guess. For each action, ask the children if they can think of a tip to go with it, for example using a clean tissue to wipe your nose, using a nailbrush when washing your hands if you have dirt under your nails, and so on.